# The Angry Poems:

## A Brooklyn Journey to Forgiveness

I0111650

## Jasmin Rivera

# DEDICATION

To Tony and Tete:
The light
that makes my life
worth living.
Mami loves you!

To ALL of the Salt Water People, Your Compassion and dedication to combatting Domestic Violence brings Pride and Joy to the Creator's Heart!
Thank You My Spirit Warriors!

When the grand illusion
of allegiance to love
surrenders to reality
All innocence disintegrates
All eyes are widened
And only faith,
will and
forgiveness
remain.

-jasminrivera-
04132014

# ACKNOWLEDGMENTS

Dear Anger,

Thank you for helping me accept the realization of the situation I was in. I know now that when expelled in a healthy manner you exist to motivate and protect the human spirit. I cherish your presence in my life and will continue to grow with you so that I may demonstrate your positive qualities.

Love,
Jasmin

## Index

# The Angry Poems
May 23, 2014, 9:09AM

Mighty molten meanings
Drip from Fire fingers
That melt alphabet
Keys
While
Wild windy words
Tempt tumultuous
Tornados
To boldly burst
From my chest
I thought you were
the best of the best
But you were
A beast whose feast
Included my goodness.
My aerial angry poems
Take target
Ejecting eulogies –
Like confetti
That waters
The dead heart
buried in
Getty grounds
That you visit
Frequently with
False flowers.

# Let Me Count the Ways
March 18, 2014 3:39am

As he stared down my soul
He plucked petals from the
Red Wootton Cupid Dahlia
And sung loudly:
"How much, for how long and in what manners can I hurt you?

Let me count the ways ..."

- I'm sick of you – get the fuck out!
- You ain't shit ...
- Your body disgusts me.
- Hope your ready for round two.
- Your a puta – I'm sure you love to suck his dick!
- I fucked her across the street from where your Mom lives..
- I can't stand you!
- I love you and I love her too, I'm torn between two women ...
- I missed your culo and your beautiful tits – she doesn't let me touch her breasts ...
- I don't want your sagging tits or pussy –
your disgusting ...

  BAM.BAM ... BAMBAMBAM ... BAM...

- I don't know what's wrong with me, maybe I will go to therapy tomorrow ...
- I'm angry that you seduced me while I was still with her.
- I don't want you to leave, this is your apartment too – we can work it out ...

  BAM.  BAM ...

## BAMBAMBAM ..... BAM!!!

- I spoke to my brother today and he agreed with me that sometimes you need something different because the same thing for so many years gets old and boring.
- She's better than you and it's gooooooood!!!
- Come here let me hug you ...
- I don't know what I'm doing ... I don't know what I'm doing ... I don't know what I'm doing ... I don't know what I'm doing ... I don't know what I'm doing ... I don't know what I'm doing ... please forgive me I don't know what I'm doing ...

## BAM

## BAM ... SLAMBAMBAMBAM ...BAM!!

- I'm sure you ran to your family and told them everything ... What's your family gonna do? Come over here and kick my ass? I like to see that shit happen.

## BAM ... SLAMBAMBAMBAM. BAM!!!!!!!

## C – R – A – C –

## K ....................................

- I don't want to press charges against you ...
- I'm sure you told your friends that I beat you up .. You think I liked hitting you?!
- Hello officer, it was just a mutual scuffle.

# Return to Sweet

March 2014

I must return to Sweet

Pink carnations

And strawberries

Must leave Whiskey fog

And Smokey breath

But it's Hard

And tempting

February melting And dripping

Down long legs

I must return to Sweet

And abandon this

New throne

But I know that

Once banished

There is no

returning home.

Two Years of
Torture and Enlightenment
March 13, 2014, 3:19 PM

I remember being naked

As the wind whipped

My body

Cold bursts that left

Life's imprints upon

My back

I sat alone

My tears turning

Into thunder

My breath a roar

and rumble

I was pulled beyond my elasticity

March and October

Transformations only

Prepared me for the

2014 Devastation.

# Feel the Poet's Pain
March 13, 2014, 3:50 PM


I want you to feel the poet's pain
The kind you feel when your cheated on
That pain that resurfaces from past abuses and oral
injuries that have
bruised your soul
Hand in hand
I want you to feel the pain of the poet's soul who took so
long to
Express herself –
Sharing the thoughts, emotions and analysis of life
That she painfully kept on the Top Shelf
That pain that pierced the poet when
She took me by the collar and threw
Me across my throne, landing on tender bones
The pain that is shame of a poet whose love was
sacrificed
for the ego of two women who
were really Mice.
The pain that is pleasure when you
Meet someone new to forget someone old
and find out that you really like them but don't know if
they like you
The kind of pain that boils in your heart when he doesn't
text back
I want you to feel my poet–pain
As this caterpillar transforms
Into a Monarch Butterfly.

# Bronx 161

March 20, 2014, 2:05PM

I sit in a parked car
On 161st Street
Pondering if you
Ever had true love.

You had none –
For me at least.

But for yourself ...
Immense feelings
Of Grandeur.

Your Ego filled the rooms
Of Our former home,
Elegantly decorated
With Blue Prints
To explore
Your Temptations
and Darkness
At my emotional
Expense.

I often wonder if
I will I ever make
Sense
Of your Selfishness?

no

# FUCK YOU!

March 20, 2014, 2:09 PM

Fuck You,
    Fuck You,
        Fuck You, ...

I write this slowly
And with purpose.

Fuck You, Fuck You, Fuck You,
    Fuck You, Fuck You,
        Fuck You, Fuck You
            AND Fuck You ...

For all the Fuck Yous
You hit me with over and
over and over again.

Fuck you for the manipulation,
Fuck you for the lies
And the years of Isolation!
Fuck You for your
Sweet nothings ! ! !
And FUCK YOU for
Saying you loved me.

# User, Looser and Verbal Abuser

March 20, 2014, 2:12 PM

User
Verbal and psychological
Abuser
Liar
Set me on fire
And held
A cup of water
In your palm.

Schemer
Moocher
Two-timing
Looser

Covered my eyes
And led me to
A plank
While you pulled
Out the shank
And gutted
My heart out

Fed it
to the Sharks
As an appetizer
before
throwing me
Overboard.

# Here is My Number ...
March 20, 2014, 2:13 PM

New Birth
Old Skirts
Thrown away
With the slip
Of a tongue
That got chopped
Out of the dragons
Mouth
Now no one
Can speak truths.

# It's Over
March 20, 2014, 4:50PM

1) It's over
2) It's over
3) It's over
4) It's over
   5) It's over
 6) It's over
7) It's over
  8) It's over
9) It's over
10) It's over

                        11) It's over    12) It's over
     13) It's over
           14) It's over
   15) It's over
     16) It's over

17) It's over .... 18) It's over ....              18.5) It's over

# Beauty Beyond the Smile
March 24, 2014, 10:33 AM

There is beauty beyond the smile,

It exists in the crease of my brow.

My beauty:

a lotus in the mud you left behind,

My beauty when with you

was that I was blind.

My shattered breast

Is beautiful too –

Shards of Sparkling crimson,

Scattered and unswept.

There is beauty beyond the smile

It exist in the rising Tsunami,

A deep naval blue that is

Uncontrollable

And destroying what

was once Me.

I was once pretty –

But now I am

Beautifully flawed.

*Monster
March 24, 2014

I once knew
A touch that
Was intimate.
An intimate touch
That became
Thorns that
Dug into my
Palms.
Palms that once
Caressed your face.
A face that
was masked
A mask
that
Was once
Removed
And what I
Saw for the
First time
I never
Want to see
Again.

## Fool's Love

March 28, 2014

The Madonna said

Everyone must stand

Alone

But I never thought

That this home

Would shatter

I realized now that

what was

Most faithful

To me

And all

that mattered

Were my delusions.

Allowed you to lead me

to the Destruction

Of my own heart.

Yes,

Only fools

Love.

# Options

April 3, 2014

Loneliness Is an illusion

That makes you

Feel closed-in,

Decide on how you want

To look at it.

I transformed

from an Eternal Girl

Into a Woman

Effortlessly

Like the Day

Turning into

The Night

On the

Eve of it's Death.

April 5, 2014, 8:14 AM

**What happens when you try to substitute a Queen for a Whore?**

> You get check mated -
> You get played.

April 6, 2014, 5:19 PM

_____

_____

_____

_____

_____

_____

_____

_____

_____

_____

_____

_____

_____

_____

_____

_____

_____

_____

_____

_____

_____

# Farewell at Full Moon

April 7, 2014, 12:52AM


My Fangs are sprouting
In a mouth
that once whispered
words of Love

My Talons are ripping
through once gentle fingers

The hair is increasing,
thick fur
An armor of my Soul

There is no turning back
At the rest of the moon -
NO ...

I'm dead
And born again new.

When gravity fails and your
floating in space the only thing
to do is reach for the brightest
stars.

April 8, 2014, 11:06AM

# What is Forgiveness?

April 16, 2014, 7:45PM

It is not stagnation?

I can forgive and move on.

It is not returning!

For I have changed

Too much to

Turn back.

It is not needing

To tell the person

Who has wounded

You that you've

Forgiven them

But instead telling

Your heart.

# April 18th The Beginning of the New Beginning

## Acceptance
April 22, 2014, 6:17 PM

I woke up crying this morning

A deep grief passing through

My Soul

left my body trembling.

Fighting to let go

of a dead past

that haunts me.

I understand now

what the phrase:

"Waves of emotions" means.

My night beach was calm

until the morning waves

of the realization

of separation

washed over my body.

# KARMA IS MY
# NEW LOVER.

APRIL 24, 2014

Today ...

I let go of the deep need for your presence in my
world.

— April 30, 2014, 1:24 PM —

# The Exploration of Therapeutic Avenues

How Can Love Turn to Hate?

"I know that I cry often …

but it is not because

I miss you

or still love you.

It's because I am

finally dealing with the

reality of the relationship,

finally allowing myself to

hurt openly without

making excuses

as to why you are

the way you are

finally crying openly

about how much you

hurt me mentally, verbally

psychologically and physically."

# Darkness

May 3, 2014

I'm in.
The realm of good versus evil
Late night battle with demons
But I still write
Swam in Agua de Florida
To cover the Inno scent
That dark creatures follow
Salivating jowls at my heals
But I still write
As I chop bush on my
journey toward
forgiveness of the pain
You caused me.

Purple-Blue clouds relentlessly
Release liquid spikes,
Piercing my psyche —
And yet ...
I still write.

As I run past
The sight of shadows
I am haunted by
"The Bond"
That hasn't broke
And yet with each key
Stroke ...
I write

My Pen
An inoculatory weapon
Turning the multitudes
Of duplicating shadows
Toward the light ...

I battle you
Every time I write.

# I Hate You

May 12, 2014, 4:44PM

People tell me it's therapeutic–
Talking about
How I feel
But I don't want
To do it
Cuz' I know
That once I
Begin my oration
I'll itemize all
Your abuses.
Wish I could vomit
It all out at your doorstep
The place you loved
To keep me as
Your emotional
Foot mat
Its only abuse if
everyday you
shove, kick
And smack
Forget about
The control of my sex,
My mind –
the thievery of my time
These are not considered
Since they leave
No physical trace behind
Of how you broke

And withered
My spirit
Only when words did
turn into action
And bones fractured
Did They see who
You really be
Because wounding
Words you so skillfully concealed
And Me –
I carried a purse
filled with pounds
of congealed
Blood
that for years drained
From my heart
They tell me
I should be grateful
For the new start
In my life
But your Words
Are still in my head
Gutting me like a knife
Telling me that I
Still have to be
The Good Wife
And continue to
Self sacrifice
People tell me it's therapeutic –
Talking about
How I feel
But I don't want

To do it
Cuz' I know
That once I
Begin my oration
I'll reveal to
all the nation
Of how you sat
At the table and ate
Away at my dreams
How you plotted
My departure
And left me with
Sorrow streams
I'll – spit – out – to – the – world
That along with that meal you
Ate
I'll serve you a desert
Of all the ways I feel
For you
Including My Hate.

# 811 Esther

As Haman was hung
by the very gallows
he constructed for Mordecai
So too
Will your spiteful actions
Be wrapped upon your neckline
Until the envy
that is yours against me
Be smothered slowly.

# A Day At the HRA

Is today your original appointment date?
What's your name?
Spell the first name for me.
Are you homeless?
Do you need a metrocard to go back home?

Hold onto your ID.
Please have a seat and wait for your name or
number to be called.

Yes, I am homeless.
I am living in a shelter
after being violently
forced out of my home,
A home that I sustained
for many –   many years.
I kept the house warm with
Love
Encouragement
Laughter.
I kept food on the table
cloths on everyones back
Yes ... I had some hard times
holding it together
but I always held my home together
until she tore it apart!

## My Soul is Bruised

My Soul is bruised
By the countless assaults
Your wounding words
Inflicted upon them
Crashing against my back
Piercing my tender skin
Pummeling me deep
Into the Earth's center
How much like your Mother
You are!
How much like your Father
You are!
How much like your Brother
You are!
A legacy left for you
By the Trinity of Dysfunction.
Sitting at your mother's chair
I knelt at your feet
begging for mercy
from your lost
spirit blows.
Have you no mercy
for this soul
that you bruise?
You remember that day?     I DO!

Papi's nena,
When you abandoned
Your spiritual children
You had
No pena.
Will you bond
With your brother?
Trade the secrets
Of the Liars Craft?
Did he help ease
Your guilty thoughts?
Did he tell you it
Was my fault?
Did he say I should
have stood
down and let
You smash my Crown?

Big brother, Big brother ...
I want to be just like you!

# Lobotomy Please!

May 8, 2014, 7:51 AM

Woke up this morning
Everyone else was
to blame
For the pain
That you caused
"Through their envy"
"For their bad thoughts"
"For their wishful thinking"
"For not telling me sooner"
"For keeping me an eternal girl"
Everyone including Me
"Why didn't you give more attention"
"Why didn't you bitch less"
"Why didn't you freak even more"
"Why didn't you stay down"
"Why didn't you lift her higher"
All I aspired
To
Was your happiness
More of what you needed
Made me less
Of who I wanted to be
I know now that
I was saturated

By childhood insecurities
Know now
That you are too
Know now
That you made a choice
To become the Monster
Who chased you in
Nightmares
Know now
That you need a woman
Weaker than you
To feel stronger
than Me
Know now
That time is
Your only hope
And my Deliverer
Today I woke up blaming
Everyone for the pain
You inflicted on my soul
But by tonight –

By tonight ...
....
.. tonight ...

I'll know better.

# It's Alive

May 8, 2014, 9:26 AM

You, Mad Scientist
Who parted genes
And studied human
Properties –
Mixed
Chemicals
In the laboratory
Of your dark psyche.
In search of the
Perfect Submissive
Breakthroughs
Appeared temporarily
As you extracted mL
Of my need
to be loved with my self doubt
And stirred

Noting the reactions:
1) "I will always live for you"
But your expectations were
Still not met.
And so you spliced
My trust and distorted
My perceptions
Placed them over
Blue flame

And watched
The change:
1) "I would die for you"
Yes! Another Mad Scientist
Breakthrough
You introduced a whore catalyst,
Waited patiently,
And wrote your analyses
As I reacted
Over and over
And over and over
again –
As you predicted.
Your experiment so close to completion
And sadistic.

But what you did not
Anticipate
Was that your deliberate
Agitation would
Awaken
A hidden trait
And as your musky lab began to vibrate
Cobb webs began to disintegrate
And I
Proceeded to mutate
From a clumpy mass of
"Yes my Love"
To a solid
Of ....

"Who the Fuck
do you
think you are!"
Electric star
Burst from
My center –
As your Mad Scientist
Experiment
Made your lab
A mess
Of promises that
Would never be
Met and
Discarded love
That would be
Eventually swept
Under the rug –
And as I stood up
from the table
And my leg became
Stable
Your eyes turned away
Not able
to witness
Frankenstein
Walk out of your life.

# Birth of Victory
May 23, 2014, 8:53AM

Today
I am victorious
I love myself
Truly and deeply
More than
I ever loved
You
Today I am victorious
I want to live
For my future
More hopeful
Than it could
Have ever
Been when we
We're together
Today I am victorious
I am nearer to my Creator
And getting closer everyday
Today I am victorious
I know my Self worth
It is          and has
Always              been
Worth                    more
Than you                  could
Afford.                      Today I
am                      victorious
I stand                          Despite
Your
a t t e m p t s
To see me fall.
T o d a y –
Victory
is my
N E W C R O W N.

# What is Abuse?

May 23, 2014, 9:56AM

What is Abuse?

How does it sound?

Does it include the silent treatment?

Is it love whispers?

- "I love you so much I can't live without you."
- "I love you so much that I could eat your flesh."
- "I love you so much I would kill you and kill myself if you leave me."

(Smile, laugh ... kiss, hug ... Laugh)

How does abuse feel?

Does it control intimacy?

Does the warm body know the difference in passion?

- "Your so hot I got carried away. You'll be alright just sit sideways"
- "It's mine so you have to give it to me whenever I want."
- "Let's do this and try that ... You can take it, you know you like it."

How does abuse taste and smell?

Are you forced to chew your words and swallow?

"If I disagree or say NO it'll be a huge fight tomorrow, a fowl mood will linger in the air for days and I will eventually give in just to dissipate the tension and have you love me again."

Give in ..... give in ..... give in ... over and over and over again. Just don't stop loving me....

Isn't abuse only hitting?

- "I don't have anyone who gives a shit about me."

- "It's just you and me baby, they're just jealous of us, of YOU!"
- "My mother this or that ... Beat me emotionally with a bat ...

    physically as a child ...."
- "They hurt me when I was a child ...."

Your job is to heal me, make me happy, fix it ... fix it ... Your job is to fix it and take it - if you really love me you'll take ALL that I dump on you .... over and over and over again ... Show me how much you love me and sacrifice some more of yourself to my insatiable need for attention and assurance ... cure my weakness...
MORE ...    MORE ...    MORE ...

What is abuse?   How does it sound?   How does it feel?
How does it taste and smell?

# Great Expectations

I never
Expected
compensation
for support
that was given
with Love - Loving Support.
I did, however,
Expect
a demonstration
of Respect,
and expressions of
Compassion
and Caring.
Now,
I Expect nothing
from you,
I Want nothing from you
and
I Need nothing from you.

# A Visitor of Love

May 29, 2014, 1:16PM

You were only a visitor
Of Love
One who entered
Into a heart filled
With purity
You spent time there
Left muddy tracks
Ate up all the food
We're rude to others
Who wished to visit
You used up almost
All of the electricity
And never asked
If you could contribute
To the bill
You were only a Visitor
Of Love
Who over stood your
Welcome
Until
You creeped out
And left
A big mess behind

**May 8, 2014, 5:07PM**

She confessed to me:
"I learned that I could maintain my youth by bleeding the innocence of spirits both young and old."

I asked her:
"Does it hurt to age?"

Her response:
"Only if you resist acceptance of karma and learning the lessons that accompany aging."

To that I questioned:
"Why do you resist acceptance of these lessons?"

Her sad response:
"Because I don't want to learn what it is like to be the receiver of selfish behavior and all of the sorrow that trails behind it."

## Pounds of Pigeon Shit

May 10, 2014, 8:41PM

Your Words are
Pounds of Pigeon shit
That you left at my door
Wrapped in lavender paper
Please take them back
I don't want them anymore
Please don't deny that
You smacked me
with lies, scared my soul
With pigeon shit words
accompanied by flies
You set me free, you did
When your eyes went astray
It only hurt because
You did it in the bed I laid
But no matter
because even
That you denied
With words filled with the
Shit of pigeons that No longer fly
But instead are fixated
With stuffing their soul with
greed, lust and pride.

# My Love

May 11, 2014, 1:53AM

My Love
was
Self Inflicted
a Dream
I injected

Our Devotion
My Illusion

Your Sex
My Addiction

What was real?

My High
On all your
tender Lies

Ohhh,
your well
Masked face
Allured me
to a
false place
I used to
call Home.

## Every Woman
May 16, 2014, 12:04AM

I was Every Woman

In my home

My collection of Hats

Was Enormous

I was the ultimate performer

For you

What needed to be fixed?

I had the toolbox

What needed tending?

I had a First Aid Kit

What needed satisfying?

I gave all of myself

What needed to be paid?

I worked, slaved

What needed to be resolved?

I talked, consoled

I was Every Woman

In my home

Until

The storm took it away.

# Denial
May 16, 2014, 12:05AM

I recently read that
Action
is the mirror of
Character
How true this is
But I often chose
Not to See the
Truth
that stood
before the
actions of others.

# Soy La Luz de Verdad
May 17, 2014, 10:34PM

I was called a Shadow by a
Gased up Pendeja
To which I replied,
"I walk with the light
And speak only Truth!
In fact -
It's the two of you
who
Have Self-Inflicted
Darkness!"

# A HOTEL ROOM AND AN AIRPORT DREAM
May 28, 2014, 1:46PM


I COULD SEE THROUGH YOUR EYES,
THE BIG PLANE AND IT'S ENGINE CLEARLY
AS THE SKY WAS BEAUTIFULLY TURNING
FROM NIGHT TO DAY,
WITH THE ORANGE AND YELLOW RAYS
BURSTING OUT OF THE DARK SKY.
WE WERE ALL THERE
AT THAT HOTEL,
THAT HOTEL THAT HAD A
GAME ROOM AND RED RUGS,
I COULD SEE THE WORKS IN THE ROOM,
SO MANY WORKS - HEAVY IN THE ROOM.
I SAW THE ROOM,
THE PARKING LOT OUTSIDE THE WINDOW,
THE EMOTION THAT LINGERED IN THE AIR,
I WAS THERE
SAW YOUR FUTURE DESPAIR
ALL FROM THE HOTEL ROOM
THAT FACED THE PARKING LOT
BY THE AIRPORT.

# Witches Laugh

May 29, 2014, 12:20PM

I finally earned my
Witches Laugh
A deep releasing
Laughter
That mocks envy,
treachery
And sorrow
A bass
that escapes
Like an earthquake
From the belly
And rumbles as it
Erupts – AHHHHHH... HAHAHAHAHAHAHAHA
A Witches Laugh
That mocks
envy,
treachery
And Sorrow
With each card that
They attempt to
Deal me
HAHAHAHAHAHAH
AHHHHHH ......

# Lucky I was Strong Enough
June 12, 2014, 12:50AM

For each time I'm hard on myself
I say, "Lucky I was strong enough"
To have known I needed to go back
to college
To have understood that I needed
To make friends -- even though
I almost lost them in the end.
For each time I'm hard on myself
I say, "Lucky I was strong enough"
To have known: remain silent
During your quiet storms
Least the monster you became
Would have been born long before.
For each time I'm hard on myself
I say, "Lucky I was strong enough"
To have planted and nurtured a seed
in the garden of my Soul for
tomorrow.
It's Root bloom today
Shade me from the pain and sorrow
Of the memories of years that try to
Rain on my mind
Lucky I was strong enough to
Stop being blind.

Its Funny
how
You cry
because you Love
You cry
because your losing Love
And
You cry
for the Love that
has perished

June 12, 2014, 12:51AM

July 5, 2014,
12:14AM
Feels good to finally let go
Feels good to finally
Realize and know
That I am victorious
And always have been
Because my heart is
faithful,
hopeful,
and without sin
The kind of sin loved
by haters and players
Who must be forgiven
Because they lack
Several thousand layers
of understanding,
self-respect -
compassion
But overflow with mastery of Lies, cheats
and deception
Perhaps, one day they will cease
the insanity, seek love's wisdom and peace
And finally know what it means to be free.

July 6, 2014, 12:42PM

It is in my nature to nurture
Hold vulnerable bodies
Close to my chest and
Whisper words of comfort
In times of uncertainty
I don't have to try, it is
Instinctive for me to want
The best for others
Even if it has meant the sacrifice of
My Self and even though
These naturally nurturing actions are
Noble
They have consequences
Especially when some bodies exhaust
Your nurturing, natural resource.
I have learned to continue to
Be a resource of nurture with
Rules and regulations so that
I have not only enough to spread
Among others but ALSO have some left
for myself.

# July 8, 2014

Forgotten
how
to laugh?
Forgotten
how to smile?
So Angry you want to yell out loud?
Waiting for bursts of joy
That can only be felt
by a child?

Take a moment
       and look Up at the Blue Sky and Pink
Clouds

That's the Creator
       Embracing Your Spirit
              Right now


And for always.

# My Poem
July 17, 2014, 4:04PM

My Poem
Is my blanket
That keeps me
warm at night
I sleep soundly
knowing I'm
warm and tight
It is also a weapon
I use to fight
I have sliced
Deeply,
In defense
of verbal
Grenades
Each word in My Poem
Steel Armor and
Bandaids
Protect and cover
My tender spirit
From enraged
Ex-Lover's
Words, touch
And abandonment
Each word in My Poem
Heals me from
All the time I

Spent
Invested in you
Each word in My Poem
Is my Mother,
My Father
As I am Created new
The words in
My Poem
Are about ME
Not you!
The instrument
I use,
My words,
Are an expression
Of my sentiments
My Poem
Is my blanket
That keeps me
warm at night
I sleep soundly
Knowing I'm
warm and tight
Always protected by
The Word that is Light!

# I Filled My Body with You

July 17th, 2014, 4:08PM

My Skin
is spelled in your name
My Heart
loved you with no shame
My Blood
pumped to your rhythm
My Eyes
contacts of your vision
My Feet
journeyed in your path
My Spirit
a clown just to make you laugh
Naive in my Virginity
I dreamed I'd be filled with your
love
for infinity
Until you emptied my contents in the
ravin.

# Seven Times Three

July 30, 2014, 5:41PM

As I lay in
My Mother's Bed
I feel the softness
comfort this
thin
weary
frame
this feeling:
Relaxation,
foreign
to my flesh,
the sweet
fresh scent
of the
White Pillow
reminding me of a
New Birth
as it
cradles
clears and
calms
my Yesterday Thoughts
...........
7 times three
means safety.

# OMG
July 31, 2014, 11:58AM

My body

Is awakening

It had enough

of death

Ready to kneel

And be blessed

Ready to swallow

Seeds of happiness

And release sorrow

Ready to ignite

life from Uterine Flames

Give birth to the Sun

Without shame

Secure my tomorrow

Ready for MY tomorrow

With a different hat

Red and Black,

Red and Black,

Red and Black

Makes me ready

To journey the right path.

## Habit
August 9, 2014, 3:25PM

I think of you often
Both Good and Bad
So that you don't die
In my Mind
Because even though
The candle burnt out
The wax still remains
Transformed in sentiment
But
Still in existence


## The Panther
August 28, 2014, 12:10PM

I am The Panther

Inked into My Flesh

Fierce and Thirsty

A consummate Huntress

I pounce my Destiny

Ravaging it to the Bone

Once done

I relish the Maroon liquid

And Tenderly bury the

Remains.

# I WANT TO LIVE!

August 30, 2014, 12:39PM

I am Alive
but
I WANT TO LIVE
I WANT TO LIVE
I WANT TO LIVE
I WANT TO LIVE
I WANT TO LIVE
I WANT TO LIVE
I WANT TO LIVE
I WANT TO LIVE
I WANT TO LIVE
I WANT TO LIVE
I WANT TO LIVE
I WANT TO LIVE
I WANT TO LIVE
I WANT TO LIVE
I WANT TO LIVE
I WANT TO LIVE
I WANT TO LIVE
I WANT TO LIVE
I WANT TO LIVE
I WANT TO LIVE
I WANT TO LIVE
I WANT TO LIVE!

# Spiritual Growth in Fire

August 30, 2014, 3:58PM

After
Being
Cleansed
through
The Fire,
The Spirit
Transforms
to
Clarity
Who
Rises
And Births
Intensity,
Generosity,
Strength,
Character,
Humor and
Serenity
So ...
Go through the Fire!
While there,
Fan the Flames,
Learn to Sweat,
Swallow Pride
And be
Reborn.

# Exceptional Human

August 3, 2014, 3:49PM

Not everyone
can be as Exceptional
As those few who
permit their
light to shine
through,
bright enough to
guide others through
their Journey
May I suggest that You:
Let your light shine
without fear
because the only
thing that the
Exceptional Human
fears most
Is the power
Of their
Own Light.

## No Doubt, No Doubt

August 9, 2014, 5:22PM

Why do I doubt myself?
When -
I have broken Chains
And have
Pumped new life
into tormented veins
I have traveled
On planes and over plains
I have Switched Lanes
And am still the same
The sane pleasant flower
That
Is built like a Light Tower
I have mended hearts
And have
Made them realize their potential
I have not yet succumbed
To the Broken Dream Bandit
I have taken much knowledge and paid
the universe back with Light
So I ask myself here tonight -
Why do I doubt myself?!

# SAFE ZONE:

PLEASE DON'T WRITE POETRY WHILE UNDER THE
INFLUENCE, MAY LEAD TO UNDETERMINED EXPRESSIONS
THAT ARE BURIED TOO DEEP IN THE PSYCHE TO
INTERPRET.

Aliens
are Loyal.
I'm an Alien,
In search of an ET
Whose gonna
Say to me:
You don't have to
Compromise
Your Sincerity
You don't
have to
Wear a mask
Allow your Breasts
to be Exposed and
Let's have
Alien babies.

## Boricua Pep Talk
August 13, 2014, 9:49PM

Sometimes I stress

Although I know

I been blessed

Was made a mess

For spiritual purpose

The attainment

Of strength is not free

So I'm content to be

In the current state

I'm in because I know

In the end

The glory will be

That the Creator wins

Over the Malo

I pray for the

Shallow-minded people

Who bump in the dark

Cuz' although I am stressed

I got the light that sparks

So, please see the lining

That's silver not gold

Because with that you

Can see how your life unfolds

Through the darkness

And the pain

Be absolutely seguro

that the Creator will sustain

The nourishment of your

Spirits

So that while

On Earth

You can be in it

To win it!

Fighting IT
August 14, 2014

They ask, "Why?"
Because sometimes it's so
full it's empty
Because sometimes the
word and action of
love
Feels void and sounds false
Because a moment of pitch
black can feel
like an eternity
Because sometimes the pain

in the soul has
no remedy
Because you can't escape
your own
memories
Because you just get so
tired ...
So tired ....
So very tired ... of fighting
IT
Everyday!

In memory of Mr. R. Williams

## Going Green in Brooklyn

August 17, 2014, 11:21AM

Going Ghetto

is not like

Going Green

When you

Go Green

You practice

Meditation and promote

pleasance

When you You Go Ghetto

You incorporate

Frankness and Vengeance

When you Go Green

You ride bikes over grass

When you Go Ghetto

You take your car and try

Run over someone's ass

When you Go Green

You call out to politicians

To make a change

When you Go Ghetto

You call the other Woman

And hit her with all your pain

When you Go Green

You want to do Yoga

When you Go Ghetto

All you fantasize about is choking her

When you Go Green

You drink things that make you

lean

When you Go Ghetto

You fight everyday

not to stay

mean

But don't get it twisted

Because when you Go Ghetto

You better know

You become stronger

And shit you went through

will bother you no longer!

I realized something about myself that I really like
I'm not a picture ripper -
Well, I did rip one BIG picture but
that needed ripping!
The rest I can look at and be okay with
The fact that it was a life I lived and I was a different person
with a different mindset -
yes, naive
But who wasn't in their past?!
It's good to be able to see how I grew in
wisdom and spiritual strength over the years
and more importantly realized my self worth
at just the right time!
I'm grateful for everyday that I am ALIVE and am humbled
by all the lessons I have learned.

And You?

_____

_____

_____

_____

_____

_____

## Dedicated to The Desert Loner

August 18, 2014, 8:53PM

In this Life

It's give and take

I give

And so much

Is taken

It's live

and

let live

I lived for you

And you let me.

Nice guys finish last

And women

Are left at

The starting line.

Times change ...

It's time to change!

# Evening Thoughts

August 18, 2014, 11:54PM

Tonight,

I hate you,

for

every night

I spent

loving you.

I cared for you

endlessly

every night

wishing now

I hadn't

and spend

every

waking day

forgetting you.

# FORGIVENESS

*August 20, 2014*


I watch Forgiveness

A Leaf

In the changing Waters

At times it floats atop

The liquid,

reflecting

A clear blue sky

At other times

I see it get caught between

Dark Waves in stormy winds

I wait for the waves

To bring it to shore.

My Mind is Beautiful
My Talent is Beautiful
My Heart has Choice
My Vision has Voice
Stay a little longer
Stay and be Stronger
As you Unfold me.

August 22, 2014

# Confidence is Built When You Arm Yourself and Enter The Battle Against Your Deepest Fears

August 23, 2014

# Today

September 2, 2014

I give up the
small brown box
That contains my fears
and insecurities
I stand at the tip
of the mountain
where the Eagle rests
and look down upon
the tops of Tall Trees
I see Winding Lakes below
that, from this perspective,
Now seem smaller
I stretch my arms and
Jump.

# Stigmata

September 3, 2014, 5:15PM

Strong Woman
Tender Heart
Bleeding Hands
Wear the stigmata
Of Eve's Lost Love
Submits pain
To her Maker
With Prayers
For Relief of
Torment
And Acquisition
Of Forgiveness

What is...?
September 10, 2014, 7:32PM

What is a Foot
Without a Shoe?

           A Farmer
       Without a Mule?

A Hand
Without a Glove?

          A Woman
      Without Love?

A Mother
Without a Home?

           An Ear
     Without a Phone?

A Man
Without a Wife?

          A Steak
     Without a Knife?

Injured,
Lost,
Cold,
Lonely,
Homeless,
Expectant
and Hungry.

## Numb is Dangerous
September 10, 2014

Numb is dangerous

Everyday is a Test

For Us

Those who

truly Love

Are always

Oblivious

To deceit,

Only defense

is numbing

Of the Hands – then Feet

And finally emotions

That if set free –

Would drown

the biggest Ocean

# PopCorn Poster Child

September 10, 2014, 9:33PM

Popcorn Poster Child

Left home to run wild

Dancing with two left feet

To abandoned

crooked beats

Hand-in-hand with

Rosey Ratchet

Who cracked your

Conscience with

Her hatchet,

Stained your spirit

with her blood

Dragged your

Rep through the mud

Oh, Popcorn Poster Child

When will you accept

This kernel of truth

Love is the Original Movie

Lust is just a spoof.

# Jailed Junked Illusions

September 10, 2014, 7:20PM

Jailed Junked
illusions
Jukebox Humming
confusions
Manic Magician of
Emotions
Mixing Plenty-Of Madness
Potions
While
Jittery Janitor Drains
False Devotion
Up Giggling Gas Pumps
Primping plastic promises
to prevent
frowns and pouts
Hoping that Her facade
will not
Be Found Out.

# Remembrance of You
September 11, 2014, 10:22AM

Every time I have to go to an appointment for HRA
to visit my Case Manager or to inquire about low-
income housing for women who are survivors of
domestic violence ...

    ... I Remember .....
What my mind tries so actively to forget.

I Remember .....
Wounding Words
Hateful Looks
Abusive Actions
The Hurt
The Pain
How Selfish you are,
Always have been ...
and the wounds tear open again.
A womb that has been trying to seal up
and recover
but as long as
I'm sitting at
the Family Justices Centers of the City
the HRA offices of my new Borough
and sleeping in Women's Safe Havens
I will ALWAYS remember you -
ALWAYS remember you
in this way!

# Coming Apart

September 11, 2014, 10:35AM

Breaking

        Cracking

                Smoking

        Packing

        Punches

For the silent memory

        That

    Yells at me in the morning

Kneeling

        Crying

             Imploring

      For rain to

Cleanse

             Wash

And come pouring over

        My weary head

      Exercise your

      Ghost from

                    My Bed
Banging
                    Shredding
                                        Pulling
               Begging
For days to go fast
                                        Further
From the past
                    Silent
                    THinking
                    Sleeping
While wide awake
                         In dreams ............
          Only I exist,
          And existed.
          Living smile -
          Filled with Bliss.

ONE,
TWO
MINUS ME
MINUS YOU
BLACK
BLUE
SKY
LOVE YOU
FOREVER
WAS
A LIE
SUN SETS
AFTER DRYING
MY FACE
THAT THE
MOON WET
OVER AND
SOBER
I LEAN
ON WINGS
THAT FLY
ME TO
NOWHERE.

# Smile

September 21, 2014, 9:56PM

Smile

So big

Filled with light

Smile

With Friends

Never so bright

Smile in

The Evening

For the

Next morning Fight

Smile

More often

So I can Get right.

## Darkness
September 22, 2014, 9:29AM

Glue,
Mask
Wind
goes past
# 1 Brush
Painted
Smile
Old child
Unraveling
From
Perished
Innocence
Sit
Stand
in Silence
Sixth day
Seven days
All days
Same
Days
Dark,
Light,
Dark again
        Dark again....
Dark
    again

## The Menacing Musicians.
September 22, 2014, 9:33AM

Cookie Crumbled
Dead Heart
Once Humble
Shivers Silently
To ungrateful
Rhythms
Played By
The Menacing Musicians
Who mumble meekly
at low bass drones
Ejected by Dead Eddie's
Saxophone
NO skat or moan left
Dried up glass
Nursed by the
Penniless
Vocalist
Whose tired of
the mess
In Her home
And tired of how truthful
The Menacing Musicians
Convey it all to the crowd
Like an Ol' woman
gossiping on the phone

# Silent No More

September 23, 2014, 10:00AM

I'm strong
I'm weak
I'm over it
I can't get over it
Yesterday
Today
Tomorrow
Hot
Cold
Night
Day
All games Played
Who Won?
One person
Two people
Third Party
Intervention
Blind
Sight
Light and then Dark
I was lost
Am I found?

Ugly
Pretty
Good
Bad
Pretend happy
Really sad
Treasure
Trash
Heart Buffet
for the Heartless
Eat away
Caring
Indifferent
Up and then Down
Truth in me
Lies all around
Tender
Violent
Never loud
Was always silent ...

Silent No More.

# Dead Meat Mami

September 23, 2014, 10:05AM

Dead Meat Mami

Cried to Bad Papi

Please Don't leave

I'll appease

Your worries

Her pain, His pain

Become grey and blurry

Papi is not happy

Mami begs

Don't smack me

Diner on the walls

Again

Blame it on the

Juice and Gin

Morning Mami

Pretends

That it will

Eventually end

And gets the family

Ready for the day.

# Soda Pop Lover

September 23, 2014, 10:05AM

Soda Pop Lover
And Musky Mate
Hover in the
Shadows
Want to
Make space
To indulge in
Lustful Ecstasy
Now that
Soda Pop Lover
Finished stealing
The Best of Me
And Knows
Just how to Remove
Lady from her
Home
Infliction of
Psychological
Blows to
Push Lady
To the Edge
In a Sinful Pledge
To Musky Mate
Needed to Clear

The Plate
For the
New Meal
Soda Pop Lover's
Conscience
Was not Concealed -
It Never Existed.


## Kitty Kat Karma

September 23, 2014, 10:10AM

Kitty Kat Karma
Roars In Rage
Perry Poetry
Is My New Age
Sage
Preparing Paths
For Fabulous
Future filled
With Freedom from
the Frightening
Fires of Your
Wining Weakness.

## My Story
September 23, 2014, 9:31PM

Moody Isolation
Gave Up
On Expectations
Remote Control
Holder
Controlled the Atmosphere
In the House
That We tried to
Make into a Home
Lonely Poems
Of a Writer
Who sat
By the Phone
And talked
To Herself,
Alone
In the Performance
Of Happiness
Wished You would
Undress
The Charade
Wished You could
Reflect
And Behave
Like Someone
I could have Trusted
But unfortunately
You Lived

for Kicks
and Lustful
Women
You Kicked
and Thrust
Me Out
of Your Life
Thought that
All the Love
I gave would
Forever make
Me Your Wife
But in dreams only
Does Forever exist,
In dreams only
Was I the Kiss
You missed
The Reality
I must Face:
I was Designed
by You to Stay
In My Place
Until You wanted
Me out of
Your Space
Silent Treatments
Always Worked
Stirring Up
Feelings
of Diminished
Self-Worth,

Starting Up
A Pattern
Of "You Come First!"
Before my own Care
Twisted My Mind
So I Never Dared
To Admit what
Was Really there
But Deep Down Inside
I Knew Who
You were
Every Time
You Grabbed
The Opportunity to
Embarrass And Flirt
In Plain Sight
Stole Kisses from
Friends Just to
Demonstrate
Your Might
Let Strangers
Suck at Your Neck
Didn't Matter
To You that
I was Upset
But that's what
You Desired
To Flame Insecurities
Into a Ragging Fire
Slowly Chipping
At My Self-Esteem

Determined to
Lick the Plate
Clean of Any
Sense of Security
I Conjured Up
For Us
In the End
You pointed
At Parts of
My Body with
Disgust
Hit Me Verbally
With Words that were
Filthy and Dirty
Sledge Hammer
Impact
Shattered Whatever
Was in Tack
Broke My Spirit
And My Bones
Threw Me to
The Street to
Fend for Us
Alone -
Looked at Myself
With Your Eyes
For far too
Long
Began to See
All the Ugliness
That You said

I Owned
Began to Hear
Your Voice
Blaming Me
For All Problems
of the Past
Even Though I
Know I was Loyal
And Busted My Ass
To Break the Cycle
of Dysfunction
That We were
Brought Up to
Practice
Wanted So Much
To Make a Happy
Relationship
Happen
So I Took All Your
Emotional Abuses
Threats of Breaking Up
With Me were
Common Uses
Denying Me Your Attention
Was also Key
making me invisible
Was One Way
You Controlled Me
I Found Myself
Emerged In
Your World

All Your Problems
Were Mine to
Unfurl
Your Insecurities
Dominated Our Lives
Going to the Beach
I was Denied
Enjoying My Beauty
Was Denied Me
As Well
Since You Were Not
Comfortable
With How You Felt
About Yourself
But for Me -
At that Time -
I Loved You
For Who You were
Enough for You
And For Me
But That Did Not
Help Your Self-Esteem
So I tried Harder
Everyday
To Make You Happy
In Every Way
Until Days Turned
To Months
Months Turned
To Years
Of Accommodating

My Time to Deal
With All Your Issues
and Fears
While I Neglected
My Rising Depression
Afraid that One Moment
Away From Giving
You All My Attention
Would Make You
Feel Lost and Rejected
You Made Me
Your Lover
You Made Me
Your Mother
You Made Me
Your Nurse
You Took from
My Purse
And so,
Here I am
Reciting These
Verses
For Others Who
Are Experiencing
The Same
Abuses and Are
Hurtin'
Class, Race and Gender
Don't Matter
When Someone
Is Abusive

It Will Certainly Escalate Farther and Farther
Don't Be Ashamed
Be Brave Enough
To Want A Change
But Remember
To Be Safe
As You Search for
A New Place
To Call Home
Don't Believe Them
When They Say
"You'll Be All Alone"
There are So Many
People Ready to
Help You Part
From An Unhealthy
Relationship
But You Have to Make
The First Start!

## Hard Lesson
October 1, 2014


One of the hardest

Lessons

In Life is Forgiveness

For so many reasons

It's difficult to attain

Even when you forgive

One day

You forget how you got there

The next

This is why being in

Daily dialogue with

The Creator is so very

Important

You ask for forgiveness

You work to understand it

And then you work some

More to keep it.


What a process!!

# Midnight Tears
October 1, 2014, 7:45AM

My Midnight Tears reflect
The glow and flecks
Of the Full Blue Moon
Shards of Steel Words
I routinely pluck from
My Breasts
Before I lay my Head on
The Chopping Block of
My Bed
Small incision at the center
Of my Heart scars over thinly
Reminding me of what selfless
Love used to be for Me
I keep my Head Up during the
Day Hours working Hard to
Empower my Self-Esteem
But My Midnight Tears reveal
To me that I still have
To Heal before I can rest from
the Fear of drowning in
The Sea I stir on rainy Evenings
When My Midnight Tears hail
Your well-packaged {sORrY}
Did nothing to avail the
Irregular rhythms that make
My Day Hours an immense
Challenge as I hide the white
Bandage strips over my injured
Spirit
But with each evening that I
Cover sorrowful sands I envision
The details of my plan to live a
Happier Life, forget the pain and
strife, Make space for a husband
now that I no longer want a wife
All these joyful wishes I pray for at
night when My Midnight Tears
Threaten to stunt my Life.

# Classy Lady

October 1, 2014, 10:26PM

Classy Lady
Once upon a time
Had a Classic Baby
Red and White flare
Good and bad stares
Her Classy Best
Calmed eradicate stress
But her Classy Dress
Began to rise
And one day
to her surprise
She became crass -
A person she
Could not recognize
So she did the best
Thing a Classy Lady
Could do
She turned About
and
Walked away
from You.

# Understanding
October 5, 2014

There really isn't much

I can do to understand it

In it's entirety

Maybe it's too big

For me to do so

Or rather, too scary

But I have to drink from

The Cup that the Creator

Has given me ...

Just as I seek to forgive

I pray that I too

Will be forgiven

Because love may

Sleep for a spell

But eventually awakens

Anew, with a wiser

Perspective.

October 2012

March 2012

December 2013

February 2014

April 2014

September 2014

# I Need

October 7, 2014, 10:14AM

I need Something
Of which I know
Not what it may be.

I Need:
A Cigarette?
Employment?
Enjoyment?
A place of Peace?
A Piece of Love?
To be Clothed?
To undress in Devoted Union?
To Speak?
To Listen?
To Sing Softly to the Ocean?
To Establish a Healthy Life Motion?
To be Grounded?
To Fly Free?
Mature Masculine Affection?
New Manners and Perceptions?
Quiet ...
Quiet ..
I need Quiet Reflection,
By Salty Winds
In Order to know
What I Need
To Begin
Again.

## Welcome Back Joy
October 10, 2014


Welcome back Joy

How long it has been

Since we have spent

Time together

You always bring

To me the Yellow

Song and Rhythm

That Opens my soul

I witness the Radiant smile

De las caras lindas

Of women who have

Shed tears that are

Now part of the Atlantic

Eleanor's Voice* reborn

In the haven that

Is Our second womb

Thank you, thank you

For your presence.

Ache

# The Past is Passing

October 12, 2014

Brand New

Blues

Not Forgotten

But are instead

In Check

Better Bet

That I would not

Remain where I

Was laid Out

Up and About

Sun Shining

Moon Bright

Spring is becoming

Eternal in my

Conscience

The Past

is Passing,

Will put away

Some change

For it's

Cheap Burial.

I Will Come Out
of this Mission
Accomplished.

I Stand

Before You

This Evening

Naked

And Unafraid

I Wear no

Worldly Cloths

But I am

Covered in

The Spirit

I've Seen You Before

I Know Who You Are

And I will not

Allow

You to Enter

My Life

And Steal

My Joy

# Out Side the Box

**October 17, 2014**

Never thought outside of the box

W
h
o
e
v
e
r
S
a
i
d

that changing oneself

e
l
b
i
s
s
o
p
m
i
s
a
w

## Rebuilding Your Home
October 17, 2014


This morning You will
Wake Up
Get out of Bed
and begin Your day
Several times throughout
Your Day
You will have opportunities
To glance at your reflection
In the bathroom mirror,
Passing by a store window,
Or
In a slow Movement
In Water.
What do you see?
Memories of actions
that You believe to be
You
But it is NOT
Just as you can decide
to walk all the way down the street
and cross at the corner
You can also decide
to cross in the middle
of the sidewalk
It's just
A Choice and Action
Don't let your actions make
You
Instead make your actions reflect
Who you want to be.

# Convictions

October 17, 2014

When You pay

Attention

To Your Convictions

You will See the Face

Of the Temptations

You are trying

To Avoid

## October 17, 2014

Frightening Flowers
Forever Forge
Fire
In Innocuous
Inhalations
That Today
Took Tired
Morning Memories
And Absolutely
Abandoned
Them

## So Private
October 19, 2014, 6:52PM


I'm Broken
Made of scraps of what
My mother thought was love
I'm deformed
Do not know who
Is a friend,
An enemy
Please God give me
Sight
Am so blind
I want love that's healing!
So why does it keep hurting?
Why do I accommodate relentlessly?
Senselessly sensitive to
The cold hearted.
Broken
So very Broken
Please,
Please!!! ...
God heal my unhealthy
Perceptions,
Fantasies that allude me
Eliminate idealizations
That rise prior to truthful
Realization.
I just want to love and be loved,
Loved in a loving way
Love ... Love ... Love ...
What is it?
Oh God, I don't know what
Healthy Love is ...
I don't know what it is ...

# UnHealthy Love Affair

*October 20, 2014, 3:36PM*

You want to tame me
Tell me what I did wrong
Shame me
I want to give into
UnHealthy submission
Live in your world
In your prison
I want to please you
UnRealistically
Move Himalayas
While your actions
Whip me
Teach me to Obey
Dominate me
Mind,
Body, Spirit
And in every way.

# Healing Poetry

October 20, 2014

Poetry
Is becoming restless,
It wants to break open
My fucking chest
Demanding absolute truth
when it comes
I need
Absolute -
100% Proof,
Can't shy away
From what It
wants to say
Shit just got Real
Prayers are being
Answered
It is now
that I will
Begin to Heal

# Sage it Away

October 20, 2014

Saged this

Soul and Body

Last night

Didn't know why it felt right

Didn't know it was in preparation

for an internal fight

Thats ALL IT IS

An internal struggle with

The Self

Teaching the self

New Behaviors

Keeping those that Work

Burning those that Don't

with Sage

with SaGe

SaGE

SAGE it ALL away!!

# My Companion

October 20, 2014, 12:05PM

My Companion
Blank canvas
Blank pages
To fill with my
Hopes
Fears
Insecurities
Joy
Depression
Anger
Thoughts of
My yesterday
Our tomorrow
No one exists
Here but Me
And my fantasies
Of a partner who
Is sensitive
Loyal
Understanding
Available
Able
and Willing
To consume all of Me
Without judgement
To overcome Me
In my Darkest Hour
To dominate
My Lust and
Praise my Innocence
Nothing exits here
but the idea
Of someone existing.

# The Cloud

October 20, 2014, 7:12PM

I feel the Cloud coming

I'm hoping it

is just

a small

storm

Please God,

let it be

a small,

quiet

quick

rain

fall ....

Indulging in dysfunction

On this purple evening,

A dialogue of analysis of

Human Behavior

with Icy Wind

Unveils my bridal passions,

Makes me lick the droplets

Of blood from Virgin lashes

And quiets me through the

Penetration of truth.

October 23, 2014

# The Season of the Fall

November 8, 2014, 5:03PM

I Fell
I have fallen
from Above
From the high Green Tree
In a New Form
Of beautiful Dying shades
of orange, brown and yellow.

When God becomes more

than a word

your language transforms.

*November 12, 2014*

# TONY & TERESA

FOR YOU:

I WILL FIND
STRENGTH
WITHIN THE
SPACES
OF MY SPIRIT
THAT I
DID NOT
KNOW EXISTED,
I WILL HEAD
INTO THE
WINDING
DARKNESS
AND LIGHT
THE PATH,
I WILL
CONQUER
THE
WEAKNESSES,
FEARS AND
UNCERTAINTIES
THAT
STIFLE
OUR JOURNEY

FOR YOU,
I WILL
CHANGE.

# The Tender Solider

December 11, 2014

The Tender Solider

Knows that the

Toughest battles

Are those that include

Those we love the most.

The Tender Solider

Will learn that one

Doesn't fight against

Those you love

but rather

Against the force

that wants to divide.

The Tender Solider

Is victorious

When she reaches

Sincere forgiveness.

The Tender Soldier

Who is the bravest

Will continue to pray and cry

Will continue to return

To the pain - no matter how difficult - in

order to

Understand,

Forgive

And reach a closer

Position to her Creator.

# Making Moves

December 11, 2014

It's time to make that move
Even if fear attempts to
Place doubt in your Spirit
Look how far you have come
Really look back today
and see how many steps
You have taken
See how much you've
Overcome!
Face the Shadows
That attempt to block
Your progress
and tell it
To kiss
your royal
Brown Ass
As you
walk toward
Your Dreams!

Be kind to yourself
As you go through
Challenges and
Transformations
in Life
because even though
You may think that
You're in control
of the next move
You fail in your
humanity
to realize that
You are but a grain
of sand sleeping
beneath
the Creator's
Immense Ocean

December 15, 2014

# Happy Birthday to Me!!

December 24, 2014

I'm turning
One tomorrow!!
I'm still
Wobbling on dirt
Amazed with
The touch and sounds
Of new things.
I hear my Father
Say, "don't touch that"
Or "be a good girl mamita"
I have not reached
The "No" stage
But when I do ...
Don't ask me for shit
Cuz' I'm gonna tell
You NO!! Hahahaha :)
I'm going to be
One
Tomorrow and
Although my growing
Pains are treacherously
Real
I am grateful
For the gift of My Life.

# Good Bye

# My Small Wind

January 8, 2015


Good bye my small wind

Your gusts were short

But enormous

I know You will return

To form a Perfect Storm

That will revive Life

january 03 2015

January 17, 2015, 7:09PM

Grateful to be alive
Given the opportunity
To thrive
To do more than just survive

enjoy my new
Found Vibe

Thank you Creator!

My Peace restored
More love in my life
Than ever before
Beastful memories
Are now ignored
Yellow Joy lights
My heart and
I Forgive and Pray
For you
Every night.

**January 18, 2015**

# Goodbye Yesterday

January 18, 2015


Goodbye yesterday

You taught me much

In the days I spent

With you I grew strong

But I am now with

Tomorrow

Who understands

The New Woman

I have become

Accepts me for who

I am

And offers me

Hope

Inspiration

And love.

SOMETIMES
WE CRY
BECAUSE WE
BELIEVE
THAT WE
LOST
SOMETHING/SOMEONE
BUT
IT IS NOT UNTIL
TIME HAS PASSED
THAT WE
REALIZE
THAT WE GAINED
A GREAT
MANY THINGS
MOST
IMPORTANTLY
OURSELVES!

JANUARY 19, 2015, 12:36AM

# Everything

January 24, 2015

EVERYTHING

Is new

Each day the past

Dies

And I am reborn

NOTHING

Remains

Only H.O.P.E.

Endures

Only L.I.G.H.T.

Survives

# No One Can Break Me

January 28, 2015

I am whole

No one can break me.

I am my own jester during

Crisis, fooling myself

Into believing I am torn

Apart as I juggle

nothing in the air

I am my own audience

Amazed at the burgundy

and gold ribbons

and lace

That color my life

I often laugh

at the end of it all

When I realize that

I am whole

No one can break me.

## The End is the Beginning
February 9, 2015, 9:25PM


You held my hand
When I tripped
Made sure I
didn't bust my lip -
But
you let me break
So I could be
Rebuilt
I'm grateful to YOU
For cherishing
My Soul
Making sure that
I grow old
In Your wisdom
And Light
I know YOU
Will be with me
Again tonight
Holding my hand
As I dream of
My rebirth in Salty
Sands
As I purge the last
Parts of a life
That was never
Fully right
I will sleep soundly
Knowing that with
YOU my Spirit resides
I was born, bathed
and now
Saved by Your Tides.

*Unless you partake*

*in the language of the Arts*

*You will not understand*

*The necessity to*

*Communicate*

*in it's many forms.*

February 10, 2015, 2:36PM

## Conversations with the Wise II
February 15, 2015, 3:14PM

She said:
"I trusted this person, I shared all I had and gave of myself just as much. I forgave even when I should not have. I prayed and worked toward the better mental, spiritual and physical health of this person. Where did I go wrong? Why was I so naive?"

To which the Wiseman responded:
"You gave Love - you did not do anything wrong. It is the other person who has to confront their selfishness, for they took something that did not belong to them."

## Rebirth
February 16, 2015, 4:24PM

The Leaf on the Tree
is Discolored
as it prepares to exit.
What reason does it
have to leave?
Because it is following
The Divine Pattern that
we refer to
As The Season
which allows
For a new Leaf to exist.
Every Leaf on the Branch
Is different but they all
Bring the Breath of Life
Upon their arrival.

# Teach

February 19, 2015

Teach

Teach

Teach

Especially

When

you

make

Mistakes.

## No More to Say?
March 1, 2015

No more to say?
You said enough!
Throw it in the trash
Along with my Love*
Knock and cry to
My Smokey Bronx Blues
Cheat and Lie
about the crack
And bruise
Spit your fire to
The two men in Blue
Crucify the memory
Of me and of you
Peel your mask
At end of day
Bow on knees
With no Honor
But shame
And pray for
That thing that
You need so much
Forgiveness
Not from Me
but from Yourself!

# Little Brown Cockroach
March 1, 2015, 9:51PM

I'm a cockroach

In your head

I crawl around

When your in bed

I flash you back

Without a light

PTSD and me

Keep you warm

At night

I squat in

Your mind

Without

Reservation

Hoping to

provoke

Your

Dark Temptation

I'm a cockroach

In your head

That remembers

That morning

When I was

So close to

Victory and Glory

And though you

No longer reside
On My street
It pains me that
You still stand so
Nobly
And with Honor
Making my work
In your head
that much harder
Sometimes I
Feel Like
I'm fading
But I'm going to
Keep trying
To conquer
Your dreams,
Going to keep
Trying to sour
Your sweets,
Going to keep
trying to keep
You with Me!

## She's Gooood!!!
March 1, 2015, 10:11PM

She's Gooood
She's Gooood
She's so Goood
She's Not You!
I want a New Toy
With The Super
Green Eye of Envy
That enjoys
Trash Talkin'
Bout you aplenty
Love when she
Gases me up
At the pump
Makes me forget
That I'm a Coward
And a Chump
She's Goood
She's sooo Gooood
She makes me
Feel Superior
To Her and to YOU!!
I'm the man
I'm the man
Whose feelin'
Gooood with her
And not you!

### Died
#### March 19, 2015, 8:23AM

# Died

# Born Again

# Revived

# All in the

# Month of Flowers

# Alive

# Living

# Striving

# Until the

# Sun Sets

# On my

# Mission.

# Que no se muere na!

March 19, 2015, 8:49AM

Doctor que me muero

Que no se muere na!

Morning Music

Motivates My

Mingled Madness

To Sanity

Safely Sustaining

Sunrises

Promised and Delivered

Meek Motions

Murdered

Bold Beliefs

Born

From Friday's Fury

That Today

Willingly Walks

Without a Care

Past Careless

Spirits.

# Lessons on Excessive Sorrow *

March 25, 2014

My lessons on

Excessive Sorrow

Made me learn

That the Creator

Has a plan for

My Tomorrow

One foot in

Front of the other

I was almost

A Mother,

I was a Good Wife,

A Sister Twice,

A Friend for Life,

But now I'm only

What I always was

A child of Christ.

# New Beginnings

March 30, 2015

New beginnings
Are decorated
With beautiful
Trimmings and
A Feast of Saints
Who lay out large
Trays of all you
Need to be saved
And shoes to walk
Away from the
Bumps and bruises
And a garment of
Many colors that
Shield you from the
Harsh elements
And the earthly lies
So walk in the
Direction of your
Transformation
And decorate your
Life.

# Conversations with Forgiveness #1

March 30, 2015, 12:08PM


- I heard the message you left on my machine last night. I was surprised to hear from you.

- I was gonna call you a few weeks back but I got caught up with some stuff.

- That's cool, we all get caught up with everyday shit. How you been?

- I'm okay. I didn't forget that I need to pick up my birthday gift, you still have it right?!

- Hahahaha!! Of course I do girl! It's been here waiting for you for the longest. When are you coming to get it Mamita?

- What are you doing tonight?

- Nothing much. Come over and pick it up and then we could go get a coffee. Yeah?

- Perfect!! I'll be right over.

# Conversations with Forgiveness # 2, continued

- I hope that you like it. I custom made it for you.

- You wrapped it so nicely ... I love the color - Blue!

- I had to send for some of the materials by special order.

- Really? Why?

- You grew so quickly. You wouldn't have fit the other stuff I had.

- Hahahaha!! I'm a tough person to shop for - so custom creating something must have been a challenge?!

- Yeah but I had fun with the new materials. Open it!!!

- WOW!! It's so beautiful. I'll cherish it for a lifetime.

- I'm happy you like it.

- You know my parents gave me something similar to this when I was a child but this is more for an adult. I Love it!!!

- It's good that you waited until now to come get it cuz' now that the weather is changing you can use it.

- Ohh your right! I wouldn't have been able to use it before.

# Brighton Beach

April 12, 2015


Oh ... what brings

The weary comfort

does not look the

same for everyone

Soft rocks

Friendly Locks

and Salt Water

hydrate the spirit,

renew vision and

strengthens resolve.

# Mirror 1:11

April 12, 2015, 11:53AM

Mirror 1:11

and the

Knees

Know no

Boundaries

In the crawl

That is Life

# Creepy Crawly

April 13, 2015, 7:14PM

Creepy Crawly

Sneaky Peaky

Think you found

Something that

Was worth stealing

Weepy whinny

Jelly Spinny

Realize now that

She was always lying

Flowing and Forgiving

Hopping happy

Glad I no longer

Have to deal with that

Crappy!

## April 14, 2015, 12:02PM
Never forget
When you run
Low on Hope
God is ALWAYS
In great abundance
Of it!

## April 20, 2015
Kindness is incurable
Joy has no vaccine
And Love is genetic.

## I Want to Go Home
April 30, 2015
I want to go Home
To a place that is in
My imagination
Taking shape and
becoming real
With everyday that
Passes.

## I'm Human
May 7, 2015

1:07AM  I collage experiences into Words.
That makes me a Poet

1:09AM  I infuse human essence with vibrant color.
That makes me a Painter.

1:10AM  I hope for Love and Cry for others.
That makes me Human

# Poem Rampages

June 1, 2015, 3:23PM


Poem Rampages

Burn Stages

That host

Blunted Babies

Who wear

Smoking Lipgloss

From their

Burning Bembas

That Suddenly Spit

Fire's Fury

Onto Ongoing

Expressions of

Agony

# Dark, Darkness
May12, 2015 4:32PM

Dark
Darkness.
ring ... ring ...
"Hello?!"
"God ..."
"... are You there?"
"Well, I just wanted to tell you that I ..."

_____

_____

_____

_____

_____

_____

_____

_____

_____

_____

"Please call me back as soon as You have time."
"I know Your busy but it's important ... So just call
me back. Okay?"

"I Love You."

**change**
May 12, 2015, 4:35PM


You said,

"change is coming."

Pennies

Quarters

and Nickels

Aren't going to

Cover this one.

I need

Transformation!

That's where

the big bills are at!

# The Busy Number
May 12, 2015 4:43PM

"Are you sure this is the area code?"

"Yeah, I told you like a million times, 777!"

I know you told me a million times but ..."

"Ayi! Look - you have to keep trying the number nena. I told you that sometimes its's a busy number! You don't listen sometimes!"

"I do! But damn is it supposed to be busy EVERY time?"

"I have to spell everything out to you?! You have to call at 7AM and 7PM everyday until you get a response!" Have you done that?!"

"No ..."

"Okay, so what you expect mija?! Try again."

# One

May 12, 2015, 4;45PM

In some
places
there are
many faces
with narrow
Heads
and
Everywhere
there
is No One
but
in the
Middle
of Nowhere
there
is always
at least
One
willing
to Help.

# Sunshine Smiles
*May 18, 2015, 10:24AM*

Shiny Bright Sunshine Smiles

Dim light burrowed brows

Mold a myriad of impressions

That delicately duplicate,

Take shape and form within

The corners of the inner Soul

Harbingers of the Light

Swing past the downcast of

Extinguishers of Esperanza

Singing songs of Our Sunday

Vociferously victorious

In their multiplication!

# My Journal

May 18, 2015, 1:32PM

I always believed that my journal was mine. Believing that blank pages were incapable of judgement, I chronicled my experiences without hesitation - until the evening I turned the page of my last entry and discovered that my journal had responded to my writing. Sentiments, analysis, questions and judgements! Yes, judgements about all I had ever written. Entries were categorized in themes that shuffled my life around as pieces of a puzzle are when one is unable to match the misshapen parts together. Page after page, in black and white, bold capped letters, exclamation points of:

Freud

Denial

Pride

Reinterpretations of long ago dreams

Blended sarcastic and comforting tones stamped my pages.


"I guess you learned that returning to the mother's womb did not guarantee that you would be born again .... well, at least you woke up in enough time to catch your rebirth!"

_____

_____

_____

_____

_____

_____

_____

_____

**May 26, 2015 9:09AM**

Switched Lanes

Plain Jane

Grabs

Bags with both hands

Moves to New Lands

Runs

Walks

Stands still

Pops the little

Pink Pill

Sleep

Dream

About tomorrow

Mix sorrow

With Joy

Shouting, "Yes Boi!"

As sleep

Turns to wake

Time to cut the

Cake fuck the pie

Made sure to teach

How the Eyes

Can see beyond the mess

How the Spirit reaches out

From Darkness

Even in the darkest hour

New Jane takes back

Her forgotten Power ...

Watch This!

# Deep Breath

June 9, 2015

Deep Breath in
Deep Breath Out
Hold my Breath
Because I taste
It's arrival on the
Tip of my Lips ...
Eat it whole and again
Exhale
Grateful to be free
Sincerely grateful
to you T
For forcing me to
Learn how to fight
For Serenity.

Best of Luck,
Be always Blessed,
Farewell.

June 30, 2015

THE LESSON

It's not even about
"Enemies"
It's about
THE LESSON
Without friction
You can't build
The Fire
That is
The Light.
ALL people
Have a purpose
In life!
Love them
Forgive them
And continue
Your Journey.

## Forgiveness Educates Anger

To believe that people are just "fucked up" is to loose your basic belief in a higher power. If our Spirits are meant to elevate in strength through Wisdom then how can we believe that people are just "fucked up" when each experience we have in Life occurs to gain the Wisdom that our Higher Power wants us to have.

www.ingramcontent.com/pod-product-compliance
Lightning Source LLC
LaVergne TN
LVHW051237080426
835513LV00016B/1632